MOSAIC

Precious Kylee Currimao Bernardo

By Precious Kylee Currimao Bernardo

ISBN:
Softbound/Paperback -978-621-495-098-0
MOBI/KINDLE-978-621-495-099-7

Published by:
Poetry Planet Book Publishing House
Rosario, Pozorrubio, Pangasinan, Philippines
Contact Number: 09554960094

Preface

Step into the vibrant world of "MOSAIC," where every chapter unveils a kaleidoscope of experiences, dreams, and triumphs. As you embark on this journey with me, allow the tapestry of my life to unfold before your eyes.

In these pages, you'll encounter the essence of "Moments," where cherished memories intertwine with fleeting experiences, painting a portrait of my journey. "Origins" delves into the roots of my aspirations, tracing the beginnings that laid the foundation for my dreams to flourish.

"Successes" celebrates the milestones along my path, each victory a testament to perseverance and dedication. "Axioms" reveals the guiding principles that illuminate my journey, shaping my decisions and convictions.

"Inspirations" offers a glimpse into the sources of motivation that fuel my ambition, while "Commitments" reflects my unwavering dedication to fulfilling my dreams and responsibilities.

Through "MOSAIC," I invite you to join me in celebrating the beauty of life's intricate patterns, where every experience, triumph, and challenge contributes to the masterpiece of our existence. May these pages ignite a spark within you to embrace your uniqueness, pursue your passions, and create your own mosaic of fulfillment and joy.

Precious Kylee Currimao Bernardo
Author

Dedication

To my beloved parents, Mr. Rolly T. Bernardo and Mrs. Josie C. Bernardo, your unwavering love, guidance, and sacrifices have shaped me into the person I am today. This book is a tribute to your endless support and belief in my dreams. Thank you for being my pillars of strength.

To my cherished family, whose love and encouragement have been my source of inspiration, thank you for standing by me through every triumph and challenge.

To my dedicated teachers and coaches, especially Sir Mark Angelo R. Damo and Ma'am Geraldyn Joy P. Fernandez, your mentorship and guidance have ignited the flame of passion within me. Thank you for believing in my potential and helping me reach new heights.

To my dear friends and schoolmates, your friendship and support have filled my journey with laughter, joy, and unforgettable memories. Thank you for being my constant companions on this adventure called life.

To my younger self (Petot) who always dreamed of writing a book.

To aspiring and budding writers and passionate campus journalists.

And above all, to God, who has blessed me with countless opportunities and blessings, I dedicate this book. Your grace has been my guiding light, illuminating my path and filling my heart with gratitude.

This book is dedicated to each one of you, for being the threads that weave the beautiful mosaic of my life.

Precious Kylee Currimao Bernardo
Author

TABLE OF CONTENTS

Chapter 1

Moments *(Experiences and Memories)*

Dusk 'Till Dawn

"Every sunset brings the promise of a new dawn."

"Happy New Year!", the townsfolks screamed with a smile drawn on their faces as the minute and hour hand of the clock landed at number 12. It can't be denied that the New Year's Eve was filled with joy and excitement, because people were looking forward for happier and better days this year 2021. There are also lists of the doings that we want to quit, which makes up our New Year's Resolution.

A New Year's Resolution is composed of our doings in life that we want to neglect, and quitting these things that we don't want, makes ourselves better. Each people's New Year's Resolution is different, due to the variety of our behaviors. But there is only one word that wraps up our New Year's Resolutions, this word is no other than, ***betterment.***

We, the children of God always yearn for betterment. Because we cannot erase the fact that we make mistakes sometimes, which is totally normal. And we want to improve ourselves and be greater than our yesterday self. And so, this is my New Year's Resolution.

"Once you stop looking for what you want; you'll find what you need." This year, I want to put in line first the things that I need, rather than focusing on just what I want. This time, I want to value and know what I really need, apart from just having unnecessary things that are just made for temporary entertainment.

"Make yourself a priority. At the end of the day, you are your longest commitment." In this point in my life, I want to put myself first than others. Because I kind of like forgetting to take care of myself while I'm cheering others up. This time, I want to know and feel myself more, so that I can develop and know what my heart truly desires.

"I'm the one I should love." At this milestone in my life, I want to give the love that myself deserves. It's not like I didn't love myself for the past 11 years, but there were times that I wasn't able to appreciate my own self, that I didn't know my worth. So as a way of making it up to me, this year, I want to learn how to value and appreciate myself even more. And I want to live on to the fact that I am worthy, I am loved, and I am enough. **I am precious.**

Last year may not be the best one, but at least we learned a lot from it. This year, it may not be the same as the past few years, but we can make it extraordinary by drawing a smile on each other's face. We may have restrictions, including the limited number of people in a gathering. But even if this exists, we can always show our love and affection for others by just observing health protocols. In that way, people will have low risk in having the virus.

I used a sunset with an opening quote because sunsets make me believe that endings can be beautiful as well. And it shows me, that even though the sun sets, when the day comes, it will rise again. It is like in life, we may set sometimes, but when the time comes, we will rise together and shine as one.

Hand in hand, we will stay together as one society, from dusk 'till dawn.

When Ompong Reveals a Secret

It was midnight. The usual peaceful and starry night was turned into a night dominated by the horrifying sound of our galvanized roof. It was a sound crafted by a drum ensemble of heavy rains which were full of rage. The whistling wind became our music of fright as typhoon Ompong revealed its authoritative wrath and clout as if it was imposing respect. The hitting of the branch of our tree on the window made every beat of my heart a soundtrack of a horror movie. It might be a haunting experience but I had a different feeling. I was irritated more than frightened. Why? The province was in a total black-out! It didn't only mean a time of darkness but it also meant a harder problem, no gadget at all!

I felt so bored at that time. I missed playing Jumpy, Everwing, and many more games that I enjoy playing a lot. I was disappointed and mad with the absence of power. I thought life was meaningless without it. We couldn't even go to the mall because of the bad weather. Suddenly, a figure came out of the room. The figure was holding a candle and forcefully exclaimed, "Let's have fun!" Well, it was just my dad.

Papa brought with him a very old wooden thing. He got it from the so-called "Baul ni Lola". Some parts of it were already dilapidated but still looked strong despite its age. Papa introduced to me Sungka. I heard that this game was a craze year back and that it involved some tricks to win. At first, I doubted and asked how this game of pebbles could offer enjoyment when in fact it even didn't have music. But, surprisingly, it was really fun! The clattering sound of the falling pebbles made a natural sound of music to my ears.

My mom also cheered us up with her all-time favorite stories. In the middle of a candle-lighted candle, she told us stories about mythical creatures like kapre, duwende, tiktik, aswang, and many more. She opened the world of imagination which turned my once gloomy and irritated eyes into an interested organ of sight. Lola Basyang, the well-known storyteller in early times, may feel insecure about the way she relates a tale.

Mom also introduced classic games such as Dama, Pitik-bulag, and many more. It was also my first time hearing funny and absurd lines that couldn't be found on Google or any website. In the morning, we cleaned and cleared some things affected by the typhoon, and at night, it was a different world for us. We didn't need any power supply to experience a night of fun and adventure. Just a candle in the middle was enough. Our night always culminated with a prayer for guidance and safety.

The power supply came back after 5 days. While most were complaining about its absence, my heart was filled with thanksgiving. When Typhoon Ompong was bidding goodbye, I resorted into thinking that maybe God sent Ompong for us to realize great lessons in life – that we need to be ready to face the worst and unexpected things, that we have to pour out the most precious time for our family, that treasures of the past have to linger on for they represent who and how we were, and that there are always reasons to continue to fight for life after a time of darkness.

As the typhoon was pivoting its way far from us, the mark that it left serves as a living reminder that we are again given another chance to savor the sweetness and sourness of living. We have another chance to soar high! Life must go on and it will always be.

The Red Skirt

Tik ti laoookkk! Tik ti laoookkk!

The usual crowing of our neighbor's roosters served as my live alarm clock that early morning. The cold breeze of December kissed my bony cheeks with ardor as if it greeted me Merry Christmas. My spirit was still in slumber, but my heart couldn't contain its excitement which awakened my spirit. I didn't like to wake anybody up because for sure it would take a long process, but then a sudden scream overpowered the silence – "Mama! My red skirt is missing!" And, they had to be up.

It was a day full of anticipation because I was one of those who were chosen to join a field trip. I wore my lucky red skirt which I wear on every memorable day. The reason behind my anticipation? It was my first time to explore more about my hometown, San Nicolas.

San Nicolas is one of the most progressive towns in Ilocos Norte. Its great development is very evident with its sprouting business areas, prestigious awards at local and national levels, as well as booming job opportunities. Its culture is very rich which is being embraced by cooperative townspeople. It is truly a town to be proud of.

We started our journey from the heart of the town. We had a tour guide at that time who explained to us the history of the Spanish-built infrastructures. We headed to the San Nicolas Church, Valdes-Ladrizabal House, now called as the Balay San Nicolas and Sta. Rosa Academy, among others. The one I was struck by the most was the San Nicolas Center for Arts and Culture more popularly known as the "Museo San Nicoleño – Buabobuabo". I had a lot of discoveries inside it and was amazed by the things that San Nicoleños had been doing and using in the past. I saw earthen pots beautifully hanged on the ceiling which serve as the trademark of our town. The write-ups and pictures elicit what a true San Nicoleño is – hardworking, resilient, and family-oriented.

After the heritage walk, they brought us to where the damili makers or potters were. We had a hands-on experience on how to make a pot and other earthen products. I found it difficult at first, but as we followed the process, I was like enchanted for I came to love finishing a pot. It was a hard process though, but this was when the value of patience and perseverance were present. We also went to Damili Production Centers, the blacksmiths, and many more.

From the journey of the past, we shifted to the modern world. We passed by the Pamulinawen Hotel, a 2-star hotel with 181 rooms believed to be owned by the elites. After being mesmerized by the elegance of the hotel, we went to the Save More for our refreshments. We also went to the Balay Condominium, 365 Plaza, Venvi Hotel, and many more. Our journey commenced at the Robinson's Mall which is now the biggest attraction in San Nicolas. We all went home with a full stomach, a fulfilled heart, and a more enhanced mind.

This exceptional experience gave me the opportunity to give importance to things in the past. We shouldn't go away from the past for these are proofs of what and who we were. These things need to be cherished and valued, and should never be buried to nowhere. In addition, this also made me appreciate more our hometown, most especially the San Nicoleños who continue to live by the values, traditions, and ancestry passed on from generation to generation. Indeed, I'm proud to be a San Nicoleño!

My neighbors became busy decorating their houses with brilliant lights and fancy decor. I was also busy imagining what could be my gift which was wrapped in front of our Christmas tree which was wrapped in front of our Christmas tree. I waited for some time and finally, the time had come. I carefully opened my gift from my parents and was shocked with what was inside. It was another red skirt with a letter of love. I felt glorious again, it meant more lucky days for me in the future.

Just after opening my gift, the usual sound dominated the neighborhood. But this time, it didn't serve as my alarm clock, instead, it was a sound of celebration. A sound of hope. A sound of thanksgiving.

Tik ti laoookkk! Tik ti laoookkk!

Positivity: The Road to Recovery

I grew up on a middle-class family, which means that we're not that rich nor that poor. But all my life, they never failed to nurture me with love and support. They've always remembered to remind me of something; "No matter what happens in life, you must keep going and think positive." Yes, it was my family who taught me the worth or value of positivity. They were the ones who made me learn that in life, bad things may happen. But nothing would ever happen to you if you were in a positive state of mind.

According to the biggest search engine in the world, positive thinking, or an optimistic attitude, is the practice of focusing on the good in any given situation. Maintaining a peaceful and positive perspective in life despite of the turmoil that we are currently experiencing has a big impact on our physical and mental health. Even though there are unexpected things that may come in our lives, if positivity is present in our hearts and minds, things will go on well.

I will never forget that time when I got into a situation where I was close to giving up my positivity. At the age of three, I suffered from a disease called “Kawasaki Disease” which is a rare disease diagnosed in every one of 11,000 people. It was a really hard time for me and my family. Because it can cause death too, which I was scared of. Every time that doctors would come and draw my blood, I couldn’t do anything but cry. But I said to my inner self that this was not the time to give up. This is not the time to stop fighting for I have my dreams which I will achieve in the future. I said to myself that I would persevere in order to recover. And yes, after spending five straight days at the hospital, I was cured and healed. My happiness at that time could not be explained. Because it is like having a second chance to live and love. Another start for a better tomorrow.

I was grateful and blessed because I always had my family by my side. They did their very best in order for me to get cured. Even though it was hard, they still stayed by my side and encourage me. As I grew up, they took care of me and always reminded me to be calm and keep positivity growing in me. Because without positivity, there will no victory. With positivity, there is always a possibility.

In conclusion, we must always look at the bright and good side of life. Amidst of all the problems that may come in our lives, we must all face it with a smile. For me, seeing people smile is a moment that is worthwhile. Positivity will always win against negativity. Positivity is the greatest way that leads you to the path of victory.

Chapter 2

Origins *(Beginnings and Foundations)*

Guiding Light

"Hope is like the sun, which, as we journey toward it, casts the shadow of our burden behind us."

In life, there is no such thing as stableness. Problems and challenges come from time to time, and we can also feel the struggle and pressure that these bring us. But who relieves all the pressure and stress that we receive? It is no other than our greatest redeemer, God itself. God is our source of strength and patience; His kindness and love keep us alive. His care and protection serve as our shield from all of the turmoil that may come in our life. He is our hope; Even in the darkest days, He is still by our side to be our guiding light.

Psalm 46:10 – "Be still, and know that I am God."

Having faith in God is like having a lifetime insurance. If we have faith in God, we can be assured that we will be always protected and loved by Him. God helps us to be a better person; a person that is mindful of what he or she says. A person that cares for not only his or her loved ones but also the people surrounding him. A person that loves each living thing, might be an animal or a tree, or anything that it could be. A person who values his life and doesn't give up even though how much life knocks him or her down. A person who believes in God. If we believe in God, we can be better, and we also can be the best version of ourselves.

John 15:12 – "My command is this: Love each other as I have loved you."

Loving others is a way to show our faithfulness towards God. As they say, we all are created equal; there is no one that is higher, and also, there is no one that is lower. We all are on the same level. And to rise up together, we need to love and trust one another. We need to hold each other's hand so that even though challenges in life tear us apart, we will always be connected through our faith and love for the Almighty. No matter how life tries to separate us, our love for each other will always bind us together even how far we are from one another. We must also love ourselves like how much we love our fellows. Because how can we love others if we don't love and value our own? Even though you have imperfections, keep in mind that our imperfections are what makes us beautiful in our own way. We are as valuable as the diamonds, or even more.

Philippians 4:13 – "I can do all things through Christ who strengthens me."

Life is not only about laughter and smiles, there are also times when challenges come for us to learn a lesson from them and be better individuals. I was just only a three-year-old girl when I was diagnosed with a rare disease called "Kawasaki Disease" which is only found in one in 11,000 people. And unfortunately, I was the one. My family spent a lot of money just to get me treated because if it gets too late it may affect the heart and may result in complications. Even though I was just a little girl back then with so much innocence, I could feel the struggle of having this disease. Day, afternoon, and night, I needed to be drawn blood for tests. I could also see the fear and sadness in all of my family member's eyes as they watched me crying because of the injections I received from time to time. After a week with the help of the Almighty, I was able to recover and continue pursuing my dreams. This experience of my taught me to always hold on and keep my faith strong in God. Because if not because of His help, I may not be able to reach what I've reached today. He is my medicine, my refuge - that will never expire and I will keep on taking forever.

Matthew 17:20 – "Faith can move mountains."

Having faith is one of the ways that we can communicate with god. Day by day, we are tested and also saved by our faith. My faith in God always gets stronger and stronger day by day. No matter how hard the situation I am in, I believe that this is one of the things that I need to surpass to become better. Even though the road is dark and rough, I believe that God has my back and will be my light and guide. We must have faith in God because He also had faith in us when He decided to offer His life by dying on the cross to save the whole world.

1 John 4:19 – "We love Him because He first loved us."

We should give back the love that God deserves. Even though we aren't perfect, He still chooses to accept and love us. Let us give back the care and strength that He always gives us anytime, anywhere. We must always remember that he died on the cross and sacrificed Himself for us to be saved from our sins; We can make sacrifices for Him by simply clearing our schedule and attending the mass every Sunday. With these simple doings, we can show God how thankful we are to have Him by our side. Life is like the sun, it may set to end the daytime and to start the nighttime. But with hope, it still rises the following day. It is like us, we may go down because of failure and spend our lives in the dark, but with God who makes everything possible, we can rise and try again until we shine brightly – in light and dark.

There Goes the Beat Again

Lub dub... lub dub... lub dub...

Everyone's heart inside the room did not seem to slow down its beat for a while. Eyes were deeply glued onto the scoreboard as if there were no available view except it. I could hear the fast beating of my heart which went even faster when I saw my mom mumbling as she looked at me. I was the top scorer with only one point ahead of my competitor. The last question was thrown and I was so sure that I heard it clearly. I was even the first to raise my card. Awarding came, "And the champion is, Carla!", announced the examiner. Obviously, it was not my name. I lost for the first time.

This was my first-ever defeat. Out of the many competitions that I've won, this was like a flip-flop. I felt like the angles were not with me at that time. With all the expectations that everybody was showing, I felt so sad. Losing for a point only made me feel more down. It was also a day before my birthday, and I considered it the worst gift ever.

My mom held my hand and comforted me together with my coach. They embraced me and whispered, "You are still our number 1". Their words relieved me from sadness. After the event, we went to my favorite fast food, as if nothing happened.

This experience of mine may not be a happy one, but it taught me a lot of lessons to live by. With the love and understanding of my parents and teachers, I was able to realize that a part of success is losing sometimes. Whenever we experience defeat, we should never consider it as the end. Strive to be better and catch the next opportunity. Life offers a lot of chances therefore we should not lose hope.

Another thing that I have learned is that it is good to hope for the best, however, we also need to expect the worst. If the best comes, be very thankful but remain humble. But, if the worst comes, accept it and still be thankful for it will surely make you a stronger individual who is ready for more challenges.

Success is the result of preparation, hard work, and learning from failure. Therefore, if we want to reach the pinnacle of success, we have to stand up from every fall – even if our knees shake, our hands tremble, and our heartbeats go fast.

Lub dub… lub dub… lub dub…

Through the Little Window

"Intayo agay-ayamen!"
Let's go out and play!

A voice took me out of my bubble. As I was busy processing the contents of the papers piled up on top of my desk, I heard a kid who excitedly called for his playmates. As I peeked through my window, I saw a group of kids, running, rushing to get to one area. Under the scorching heat of the sun, they were happily playing, and their laughter echoed throughout the neighborhood. And suddenly, I was a child again.

Before I had a lot of responsibilities that I had to think about all of the time, I was once a kid - innocent, careless, and easygoing. A kid who would instantly go out after being called by her playmate. A kid who never cared if her clothes were soaking wet due to the excessive amount of sweat. A kid who would skip and jump high, bend low, and run fast, just to win a game. I was a kid who grew up loving to play traditional games, or what they call it, Laro ng Lahi.

A huge number of athletes from the Philippines have dominated the international arena and have successfully raised the country's flag high in various sports events. There is no doubt that Filipinos have excelled in different sports. However, if we go back in time, it cannot be denied that it all started with the Laro ng Lahi - where Filipinos were given the chance to play, enhance their skills, and observe sportsmanship, for the very first time.

Before Filipino athletes learned how to play archery, billiards, bowling, and the like, they first showcased their accuracy and precision by playing **Tumbang Preso**. They would think and plan about the best angle to strike the can. Focus and accuracy would be seen in their faces, as they want to emerge victorious in the game.

Before soccer, basketball, and the like, Patintero honed their collaborative and coordination skills first. In **Patintero**, they had to tag or pass their opponents. The skills used in Patintero are similar to the basics of playing the aforementioned sports, for the players need to measure every bit of their moves and know when to run, when to catch, and when to shoot or goal. To work as one, and to win as one.

We also have the Palo Sebo, Sack Race, Tug of War, Luksong Tinik, Luksong Baka, and Piko, which teach players to be resourceful and creative when it comes to their game tactics. These also show the importance of physical fitness, including one's body coordination, agility, and speed.

Given all of these, Laro ng Lahi played a vital role in cultivating Filipino athletes from one generation to another. It may not be as fancy and grandiose as other sports, but it ignites our fighting spirits and reminds us of who we are - we are true-blooded Filipinos, driven by courage and determination to bear the brightest torch and to bring glory to our country.

No matter where life brings us, may it be on the top, in the middle, or at the bottom, may we never forget the cultural roots that made us the resilient people we are now. All of us were once kids, enjoying the wonders of our childhood, making memories that are for the books. In a world wherein there are endless tasks and inescapable responsibilities, let us allow ourselves to take a break, to take a deep breath, and to reminisce about the good old days. Let us embrace the comfort and nostalgia brought by the Laro ng Lahi, which makes our inner children happy and keeps our minds and hearts young.

As the nostalgia came to an end, I was taken back to reality. I could see that the children were already tired and worn out from their games, but their smiles never disappeared. As they were taking a rest, I found myself smiling, amazed by the refreshing sight I laid my eyes on. Truly, Filipinos are optimistic, and will always take pride in what makes them happy and what makes them better individuals.

"*Ton bigat manen!*"
See you again tomorrow!

KARISON: Where Will Hope Bring Us?

The sound of morning roosters shatters the silence of dawn. The sun rises from the multitude of clouds covering the vibrance of its rays, signifying a new day. As the sunrays start hitting the land, Nestor, an Ilocano traveler sat on the back of his carabao pulling a karison, reaches his hand to his straw hat to shade his head against sunlight. After a good night's rest from traveling from Batac to the heart of the province, Nestor starts his day with a prayer of hope as he is about to embark on another journey that he believes will make the life of his family better. He is one inspired Ilocano dreamer, who had decided to leave the comforts of his home and province, to seek new opportunities at the capital of the country, Manila.

Every Ilocano is a Nestor – they are always ready to make sacrifices just to provide for their family better. They are willing to do anything to make ends meet to serve food on their dining table. They are dedicated to taking on a challenging journey as long as this leads them to success. As Filipinos, we have traversed through many oceans and have taken different roads with hopes of finding a more progressive life. We've gone through many tour guides who promised us a destination wherein freedom and equality will finally be within our reach.

In this modern society, wherein it can be hard to decipher if something is real or just sugarcoated, the spread of false hope can be very rampant. Filipinos who want to make a living to make sure that their families are well sustained are deceived by sweet lies coming from people sitting above. However, a Filipino who knows his principles remains steadfast and possesses the desirable values to achieve real change. These will guide them throughout their whole journey. With these, their dreams will turn into reality, and no such thing as false hope will hinder Filipinos from growth. With these, they will know when to PEAK.

Filipinos know their PURPOSE. Being considered warriors, Filipinos never enter a battlefield unarmored, and most importantly, they never leave a battlefield until they win the battle. Some may underestimate the capabilities of Filipinos and say they're weak, but Filipinos prove them wrong over and over again. Filipinos will always make them remember that they will fight for what's right and what's theirs. With the love of their families and the support of their fellow countrymen who serve as their shields, they are empowered to leave a legacy wherever they go. They know why they are on that battlefield – to win, to bring change, and to uplift our nation.

Filipinos are the primary advocates for EQUALITY. Being deprived of rights and being held by the chains of poverty will never stop them from seeking justice even against the privileged. As Filipinos, we know that the trails of greed and corruption don't flow in our veins. Instead, the values of unity and integrity become the oxygen that causes our hearts to pump. Even though Filipinos come from different bloodlines and have different social backgrounds, they are bound by one string – the string of nationalism. This string doesn't care about belonging to high or low ranks, or how much money one's bank account contains. It looks for pure love for the country and its people - love that doesn't oppress, love that doesn't harm, love that doesn't dictate.

Filipinos are ADAPTIVE. The world is fast-changing and it is a good quality of Filipinos to be able to embrace change. However, they don't let these changes make them forget the pain of the past. Instead, they use these changes to make sure that the future generation will become firm but malleable, adaptive but not easy to manipulate. Filipinos are adaptive in the sense that they can make the best even out of the hardest days. They can carve a way to success out of the piled-up hindrances. They can initiate a movement to put our nation to the pinnacle of success.

Lastly, Filipinos are rich in KNOWLEDGE. It is not only in books that they learn from but also their experiences. With their knowledge, they can prevent history from repeating itself and save their fellow Filipinos from tyranny. They will be able to make decisions that will benefit their family, even though it means sacrificing some things. Their knowledge will help them to steer their boats in the stormiest of seas, provide them shade in the hottest of daytime, and give them light in the darkest of nights. This knowledge gets passed on from generation to generation, which will result in a beautiful harvest of excellence.

Despite the accomplishments of our country, are we traversing the right way? We have to make sure that we are progressing not only in the financial aspect but also in the governing bodies and mentalities of the people. In terms of public relations and economic development, there are changes. However, when it comes to our justice system, is there no room left for improvement? We must remember our purpose, fight for equality, remain adaptive, and use our knowledge to spark change for a better Philippines. It is only through our initiative that our country will not surrender to other countries, be smeared with blood and violence, and let crocodiles feast on our hard-earned success. It is time to make a move, let our voices be heard even at mountain peaks, and pick the right leaders.

After passing through the bumpy roads, Nestor finally gets to his destination at the población. As he bids goodbye to his Carabao, he reminisces about the journey of venturing through the scorching heat of the sun and the cold rainwater. Nestor freshens up and checks his bags and supplies. He was about to enter the bus when he suddenly went back and grabbed his hat made of straw. He decided to bring it with him. It was all eyes on Nestor who got inside the bus holding his straw hat close to his chest, but Nestor didn't mind even a single stare. It was easy for the other people to judge the exhausted, simple-looking man who got inside with bags nearly ripped for they didn't know what he went through. But that poor-looking man, who had his straw hat attached to him, valued every drop of sweat and every step he took just to get in there. And he will use that same determination and appreciation to do well in the big city to be able to serve hot meals for his family. If every piece of hard work and dedication exerted by the Filipinos are valued, then the Philippines would have regained its spark and joy, and Filipinos would have seen where their fervent hopes could bring them.

Chapter 3

Successes *(Achievements and Triumphs)*

Metamorphosis

"A good education is a foundation for a better future."

Education is known as the key to the threshold of success. It helps people to achieve their dreams and serves as the answer to all questions. Education, when taken seriously, provides a beautiful future - not only for you alone but also for your family and friends. Education is an important factor in living a genuine life. With education, people can understand and know what's going on, people would know how to make decisions and learn how to live a worthy life.

The 13th of March was our last day at school. I can still remember by then because it was also exactly my birthday. We were so happy that time, we were always. After my birthday party at our classroom, everyone bid their goodbyes, expecting to see each other again the next week, because that was our routine. Suddenly at night, a news flash was shown on the television screen saying that the classes were suspended for a couple of months and going out was temporarily prohibited. At first, people could endure it and thought that it would only go for months, but nobody expected it to turn the opposite way. Minutes turned into hours, hours turned into days, days turned into months, and months turned into a year.

Because of the pandemic, the whole country, and the whole world was put into a lockdown. A limited number of people could go out, by schedule. The opening of classes was approaching, and students had no idea how they would continue their education despite the situation. That's when Printed Modules and Activity Sheets came into the picture. It was said that the grades of students would be determined based on their scores on these papers. Little did we know that these papers would change our lives in this current situation.

I have always been an honor student, and I admit that it can be pressuring sometimes. It was difficult in the past face-to-face classes, and when it turned to Online and Modular Learning, it became harder. It was hard for many students to adapt and adjust since they were used to the typical face-to-face classes. Students were not used to seeing their classmates just on screen when in the past, they would laugh and smile a lot. But having to experience this for a whole school year, students finally adapted to virtual learning.

In this current learning system that we are on, it doesn't only need intelligence in order to have good grades. It must be accompanied by hard work and patience. Intelligence is nothing without actions. Strive and try to do the assigned school work. Read the given printed modules, don't just settle on Google. Attend virtual classes, in order to understand the lesson more. We haven't experienced it before, but it doesn't mean that we can't learn and get help from it.

Yes, it is true that grades don't define who we are or what our future is, but good grades will help us achieve our dreams and make us what we want to be. It is hard, especially now that we are stuck in our own homes, but let us always remember that the storms in life don't always last that long. As long as we do our best in our studies and in following the health protocols, we can slowly change the world. The world may not heal later, it will not heal tomorrow or in the next month, but it will surely heal soon.

Also, let us not let our studies destroy us. There had been a lot happening to students due to the amount of schoolwork given to them. If we get tired, let us learn how to rest and not to quit. Besides all of this negativity, this situation taught us how to be independent and strong. It taught us how to grow alone. It made us grow in all aspects; physically, emotionally, mentally, and others. It made us deal with problems more properly. And it also gave us the chance to know and get closer to our family.

According to Abhijit More and I quote, "A man without education is like a building without foundation". Let us build our future strong and persistent. Most especially, let us build ourselves into a determined and firm one. We are the passport to our success, along with education. And so, as we go on and on to the higher levels of education, may we always keep in mind that this perseverance of ours will pay off in the end. Let us keep our fighting spirit burning, and strengthen our faith in God. Let us grow together, hand in hand.

Held by the Chains

I was always a dreamer. A dreamer with an extraordinary vision, who yearned for things people considered a burden. A dreamer with a strong grip of commitment and confidence, who stood up for herself when everybody was pushed down. A dreamer with a loud voice, which roared from the lowlands to the highlands, never letting anyone or anything silence it. I was always a dreamer. An explorer of things yet to be seen. A pursuer of tasks no matter how hard these may seem. I was a dreamer. Now, I'm a journalist. A fighter.

I enter the room with my pen and paper in hand, with everybody's heads turning to look at me, suddenly examining my whole presence in just a snap. I proceeded to approach the front seats, and I could hear murmurs of individuals at the back. I would love to listen, I would love to make an answer. However, my attention is much more needed by the scene right in front of me. A man being charged with the crime of murder was about to be interrogated. I quickly removed the cap of my pen with the tip of my finger and started jotting down notes. I gathered data and statements that came out of the interview, and I got ready to broadcast and update the country.

I appeared on camera with a straight face, not even a trace of emotion left behind. My task for today was done, and I was able to finally go home. I opened the doors of my house and was greeted with a deafening silence. I roamed my eyes around my empty home, looking so dull and lifeless. The home that used to be filled with laughter and brightness, was just a constructed building with dim lights and lost hope. I closed the door of my room, and tears fell down like a waterfall. The journalist who reported the news, looking so composed, was bawling her eyes out due to the struggles life has given her. The journalist, who was always seen as fierce and unbreakable, wept because of the tragic death of her mother, the victim of the said murder.

It broke my heart to see my mother's killer up close with no sign of mercy or regret left for the love of my life. I wanted to scream. I wanted to make a scene. However, because of my so-called dream, I will never have the chance to avenge my mother's death. With the neutral image I'm required to maintain, I know that I will never fight for the justice my mother deserves. As much as I would want to shout to the world that the man is guilty, that he unmercifully took the life of my mother, I needed to suppress my voice. I needed to wait for justice to be served bit by bit, hoping that it would favor our side.

I lost a major part of my life when I lost my mother. The woman who patiently built me. The woman who encouraged me to reach my dream. The woman who brought me to the pinnacle of success. The woman whom I loved so dearly, had disappeared. Now, my life's not the same anymore. The vision that once saw a good future ahead was shattered. The strong grip that once had control in my life gradually loosened. The voice that once echoed in every corner of the room was silenced. I couldn't find the right ink to start writing with my pen. I couldn't find the light that would show me the way. I couldn't find myself and my will to live.

After long days of recovery, I've finally found the purpose in my struggles. The death of my mother and the crime committed by the killer may have altered my life, but this has served as a challenge to me, as a journalist. This heart-wrenching situation must never be experienced by anyone ever again. And so, I will do my best in my duty to broadcast the truth, and nothing but the truth. In my chosen field, journalism, struggles, and risks are inevitable. However, I will always believe in the radiant torch of journalism, raised high, emitting light beyond horizons.

I was once a dreamer. Laying out my plans orderly made me think that my future was already aligned. But, no, things really do happen sometimes. Our problems might create a cloud that covers the sun that shines. However, a rainbow will eventually appear, a hopeful future, it reminds me. Throughout my hectic years in the field of journalism, I've learned one great thing - to accept that the world is a work in progress. It is important to see the beauty in everything, and that there is beauty in you, amongst the turmoils of life.

A fighter, like me, will always do her best to give justice to a dreamer, like you.

Hold on, Voyager!

A journey towards a dream starts with one pen and paper, one teacher, and of course, one student.

Students are voyagers trying to navigate their way across the wide ocean full of challenges and travails. Despite the harsh rains and waves, they hold on tightly to their ship, strive to direct it to its proper destination, and never let the currents of the ocean take away their courage and determination.

It takes a lot of effort in order for these voyagers to be captains and conquer the ocean. A lot of obstacles are sent to interrupt their sail - the scorching heat of the sun brought by high expectations, the never-ending change of weather that symbolizes their yearning for validation, and the lack of warmth during the coldest of nights because of self-doubt.

Trying to navigate their way across the vast ocean is not an easy task. They have to burn their midnight oil just to attain a round and gold medal that they believe will serve as the light that will guide them throughout their voyage. They have to sacrifice a lot of their time for themselves, just to understand the lessons and earn high grades, that they believe will give them ample knowledge to sail. They have to dedicate their blood, sweat, and tears, just to make their parents and loved ones, whose expectations and hopes are evident, proud of their hard work and appreciate them for making it this far.

Dear voyagers, may you not lose the drive to continue traveling until you get to your heart's desired destinations. The sun may shine too bright for your eyes and might hurt your skin, the rain may pour and drench your clothes, and the wind may blow toughly, but you shouldn't stop sailing. Hold onto your goals. Hold onto your heart's whisper. With your strong determination, the stars will align and guide you toward your journey to success.

You can never tame the waves, but you can always go with its flow. Students, keep your heads up. You still have a long way ahead, but you have gone this far - and that's amazing. There's always a time for everything and for everyone, never think that you're alone and left behind. Continue your adventure, and may you sail with flourishing colors.

Chapter 4

Axioms *(Values and Principles)*

Living with Pride

We cannot always build the future for our youth, but we can build our youth for the future."

Such a powerful quote shared by a powerful person himself, Franklin Roosevelt, which clearly manifests the great essence of molding the youth for the future. With the existence of the super-information and communication highway, it is disheartening to note the fact that some youth tend to forget the significance of preserving and caring for one's culture. They don't recognize its role in shaping identity. Because of this truth, it is now an indispensable goal of every community to advance the young people toward a creative which is culture-inspired.

Creative economy by definition deals with the interplay between economy, culture, technology, and social aspects. It has become a trend in the global economy to keep pace with the ever-transforming world while cultivating creativity and keeping culture intact. Why is there a need to involve the youth in such an endeavor? What character traits has the youth that may lead to a victorious outcome? Let me stress to you an acronym filled with meaning – I CAN.

INTELLECTUAL. The youth are considered the most intellectual ones when it comes to creative tactics. Their minds are so fresh and they have the great capacity to absorb teachings very fast. With their considerable knowledge in the field of research, they can make their minds an avenue of wonderful creations. They have the power to turn an ordinary thing into an unimaginable, extraordinary one.

CHEERFUL. Cheerful in the sense that they are happy workers. They do what they love and once they are given tasks that bring out their ingenuity, they will surely accept the challenge. The government as well as the schools should then give the youth various opportunities that could test their creative skills while displaying Ilocano culture. Exhibits, art competitions, and workshops, are some of the many activities that may be made available. In my hometown, the Damili festival calls for a huge rate of youth participation through dances, pageantry, and songs, while displaying the culture and heritage of San Nicolas. And yes, even after a rigid practice, the Ilocano youth still projects a jubilant smile.

ASPIRING. The young ones are the most active and emphatic members of the society. They are risk-takers, have high spirits, and are goal-getters. They aspire to be better and are very competitive. However, they still should be given much guidance from the adults and the parents for their eagerness to try new things may compromise their future. While the youths are daring, the adults are and should be caring.

NEGATIVE COMBATTERS. The youth have a very positive outlook in life and in their positivity brings them to places. A positive attitude in the achievement of a goal serves as a motive to go on despite of how difficult the task is. Failure is inevitable; however, life is full of chances, they say. The youths have the biggest opportunities that can lead to a successful and comfortable life. Dr. Jose Rizal expressed his high expectations for the youth when he considered them as the hope of the fatherland. He was never mistaken after all.

As the nation is being faced with a lot of complications, the Ilocos region gives its full confidence that through us, the Ilocano youth, it can achieve its goals for a prosperous community with productive, creative, and value-laden citizens. We should live with the treasures from the past, move for a bright future, and survive for a fruitful today.

The Ilocano culture is the reflection of the beliefs and identifiable traits of a true Ilocano, therefore it has to be conserved and safeguarded. The youth has the greatest role in its preservation and serves as a key to opening the threshold of success. As an Ilocano youth, with confidence and pride, I say, I CAN! You surely CAN! Together, we CAN!

GAPAS: An Ilocano's Harvest of Hope

The clock strikes six and the sound of the morning rooster awakens me. As I get pulled out of my deep slumber, I am greeted by the bright rays of the sun hitting my face, the cold breeze of fresh air causing my hair to sway. I make my way into our kitchen and find my grandfather preparing to go to the fields. The aroma of his coffee, accompanied by the great smell of the hot cooked *sinangag* filled the air, signifying another beginning. My grandfather tells me to settle down and eat, while he grabs his hat made of straw, bidding me goodbye. *"Innak 'diay taltalonen, nakkong. Sapay kuma ta makagapas kamin."*

This was the life I was born into. Raised by farmers, the value of gratefulness and seeing the good in everything had been instilled in me since day one. I have always considered farming as an act of hope - from plowing the land; planting the seeds and crops; harvesting the fruits and grains; to selling it for a reasonable price, which is a testament to the optimistic personality of farmers who exemplify the qualities of an Ilocano. Not only that, I have learned that hope comes in many forms - Hope is envisioning a brighter tomorrow amidst the uncertainties that we face day by day. Hope is like seeing the dark clouds making way for the shining sun. Hope is believing that a seed can grow and thrive regardless of the droughts or storms it may encounter.

Ilocanos are like seeds. Planted in this world, raised by the gentle hands of their parents. Nourished by the diverse and beautiful Ilocano culture, shaping their minds and embracing their identity. Storms may come to test their strength, try to knock them down, and shatter their dreams. Droughts may occur which will make them feel tired, out of chances, and on the verge of giving up. However, they, being true-blooded Ilocanos, withstand the different seasons that come in their life. When a storm comes, they prepare and secure themselves and their homes. They remain steadfast as if no battle can defeat them. In times of drought, they make a garden of love in their hearts, remain hopeful, and seek God's guidance. Nobody, nothing can bring an Ilocano down.

The good qualities of Ilocanos get passed down from generation to generation. The concerted efforts and dedication to cultivating the seeds cause a seedling to sprout. It's similar to us, Ilocanos. When we dedicate our time to the betterment of our lives and society, we are able to make a better place for our youth. They are the seedlings of today's generation. They are the manifestation of the summed-up passion and willingness to serve the country and help it progress. Oozing with wit and enthusiasm, there is no doubt that the youth can help in nation building, providing avenues to hope, freedom, and justice. Just like how seedlings need care in order to grow, the youth also needs care and attention in order to be the best version of themselves. We must support them, cherish them, and acknowledge them.

A seedling, when it is well taken care of, grows into a tree that bears fruit. It had endured lots of challenges, weathered by the scorching heat of the sun and soaked by the cold rainwater. It's not just a tree standing tall, but it is a tree that provides shade for people, becomes a resting place for the tired, and has got a lot of stories to tell. Just like Ilocanos. We have gone through so much, but here we are, full of hope and standing with pride. Even though there are a lot of challenges, judgments, and threats that have been thrown at us for years, our hearts are still beating, our veins are still filled with the Ilocano blood, and our smiles show that we are proud to be Ilocanos who started as a seed, strived as a seedling, and now bearing fruits as a tree. Truly, the rain gets poured on people who really deserve the sun.

After a long tiring day, my grandpa returns home. I could see on his face his happiness; I am guessing that they had a great time at the farm. I quickly ran to him and hugged him. He was hesitant at first, for he thought I would complain about his smell. However, I told him that I didn't mind. Never in my life, I felt ashamed of having a farmer as my grandfather. I didn't mind the dirt in his hands, nor the earthy scent that clung to his cloth. I was proud of having one of the backbones of the country's economy as my grandfather. I couldn't and wouldn't ask for anything more. And yes, they had a bountiful harvest.

The Dunes of Hope

When coming to Ilocos Norte, enjoying the beauty of both the natural wonder and memorable experience in the Paoay and La Paz sand dunes is a must. The pale-yellow sand that amazes everyone with its steep slopes and scenic view especially when hit by the rays of the sand dunes has two elements significant in the realm of sports - the wind causing your hair to sway, and the smooth refined sand beneath your feet, signifies the setbacks and breakthroughs encountered by every athlete.

The powerful wind blows symbolize setbacks in their athletic journey. They may feel discouraged as they might lose their track and balance, but with their love for sports, they remain steadfast and believe in themselves that they can do whatever it takes just to triumph. They undergo months of training and follow rules physically and mentally just to hone their skills and condition themselves to be deserving of a medal or a trophy.

The smooth sand beneath their feet symbolises their hard-earned athletic breakthrough. After overcoming challenges and defining the odds, they get a taste of their sweet success and use it to further better themselves. The grains of sand beneath their feet are their sacrifices and efforts, countless, and provide support, which is the reason why they are standing with pride. Their dedication to sport and open-mindedness to their coaches became their wings to go and reach the pinnacle of success.

Hope can be found in everything - may it be the ball you are holding and kicking, may it be the bow that you let go, or the field and the water that you run and swim into. In sports, hope comes not only in trophies or plaques but also in hearts overflowing with commitment and belief in oneself. Hope is found in the sun, in the sky, and the dunes.

Indeed, hope conquers all.

Life's Basketball: The Ilocano Resiliency

Basketball is a popular sport in the Philippines. As everyone's favorite pastime, basketball paves the way for building harmonious relationships between players and instills in them the values of camaraderie and sportsmanship. The impact of basketball in every Filipino's life should not be confined to the four walls of the basketball court but should extend to reach the deepest creases of their hearts. It is through the skills and the real essence of basketball that we, Filipinos, will develop resiliency and capture the gold for our collective victory.

There are skills that basketball players take months or years to practice to be able to play excellently. The basic basketball skills such as passing, dribbling, and shooting, are key skills that will hand over the trophy to the players. At one glance, these don't seem significant and are only mere gestures used in basketball, but when viewed from another perspective, these can be applied to our day-to-day living wherein we also try to win each day.

Passing. There are times when a basketball player is doubting the probability of him making a shot, that's why he chooses to pass it to another player to not waste the chance. It is similar in real life. There are times when we aren't sure whether we will make it or not, but instead of tossing it in the trash, we give the opportunity to those we know deserve it and will make the best out of it. This magnifies the value of humility. In life, we can't have it all. That is why we let go of some things and let others have it. At the right time, a greater opportunity will come and will take us to greater heights.

Dribbling. When a player dribbles the ball, he has the determined hope of shooting it. He runs fast, debunks the techniques of his opponents, and protects the ball. So is life. If we have a dream, and we want to make it come true, we hold onto that dream firmly, defy the odds, and go above and beyond to take it to realization. This highlights the value of determination. We, having high dreams, is not surreal. We have the freedom to do so. And we are responsible for making these come true. So, let us just dribble, and dribble, until we reach the high ring to shoot.

Shooting. Not breaking their momentum, the players successfully pass through the obstructions made by their opponents, aim properly, utter a silent player, and shoot! In life, we have overcome many challenges and exerted much hard work to get to the pinnacle of success. We seize the moment, aim our plans, and shoot our shot. This emphasizes the value of resiliency. No matter how hard the road is, we endure it like a pot being fired to ensure durability. We do everything we can to arrive at our desired destination.

The value of basketball doesn't end with the loud cheers and whistles but continues to live through the values of humility, determination, and resiliency. Our fate is in our hands, our life turns out the way we want it to be. In order for us to get the best out of our goals and aspirations, let us be passionate and disciplined like basketball players who never give up until they lay their hands on the trophy.

Keep on believing. Keep on working. Keep on shooting!

Chapter 5

Inspirations *(Sources of Motivation)*

The Angel's Song

"Kiss me, kiss me, in the morning…

Kiss me, kiss me, in the night…

Kiss me, kiss me, in the daytime…

Kiss me, kiss me, all the time."

The usual singing in the kitchen serves as our alarm clock every early morning. I am always anticipating it because this offers us a fun feeling. Whenever I hear it, my heart goes thumping as it makes me appreciate being loved by my loved ones. It is also a time for bonding between me and my favorite grandma, Lola Manuela, whom I call "mommy".

My grandma is one of the best gifts life has given me. She is considered as my companion whenever Mom is not around. In reality, I first thought that she was my mother. I love everything about her – her funny quizzes, her absurd stories, and not to forget her captivating voice that melts the heart of the listener. I could not imagine myself growing up without her. She is my everything.

What I can't also forget about her is her teachings in life. I may not be able to understand what she's discussing, but I'm still all ears because I know that she is just thinking of my own good. She was the one who taught me the secret of winning, but when losing comes, acceptance with thanksgiving, according to her, should still reign.

One day before the cold breeze of December touched us, I heard a different tune in the kitchen. Instead of the common joyous melody, it turned out to be a gloomy piece. Though I was still dozy, I jumped off my bed and saw a heartbreaking sight. Grandma and her children were hugging each other while bursting into tears. I knew it, grandma was leaving the country for good.

I felt so devastated at that time. It meant no more funny stories, no more words of wisdom, no more early singing. I hugged her so tight and cried hard. Who will be with me when Mom and Dad are out? Who will cheer me up when loneliness strikes? How will I overcome my fears? As I was sobbing, my grandma lifted my face and smiled. She explained to me that she was leaving not because she wanted to, but because she needed to. She again left me with thoughts that in life, the only permanent thing is change. And that whenever change comes, we have to accept it. Love will always bind hearts wherever point in the world they may be.

Seven years have passed, and I've realized that every word that my grandma uttered was true. Distance is never a hindrance to showing how much you care and love someone, for love will find a way.

A familiar sound overpowered the silence in our kitchen. It's again that fun-filled song being sung by an angel on an early Saturday morning. I felt so excited and ran towards that sound. It was my Lola Manuela on a video call. Well, it was not what I expected, but I felt more loved for even though she's far, she still seems so near. I sang with her just like how I would do when she was still here. Perhaps, I will never long for that angelic voice again.

"Kiss me, hold me, hug me, darling, with all your might."

What is Behind a Hero's Cape?

When I was a child, my perception of a hero was someone dressed in a suit, his cape draping over his back, a ray of light following him wherever he went. I used to think that a hero was someone who possessed a special type of power that was made to fight extraordinary creatures that brought burden to the nation and its people. The hero would lift himself up and fly, and in just a blink, the villain would defeated. As my innocence gradually fades away, I've come to realize that victory cannot be achieved easily. No such hero wore a cape and had a light following him in places he went to. The heroes of the real and modern world weren't given special powers to combat evil, rather, a pen, a microphone, or a paper, was found in their hands.

They have with them their bleeding pens that continue to search for the truth. Their mighty voices can never be silenced by either money or a gun. Their papers can never be torn apart by an iron hand. They are the epitome of resiliency and hard work, they stand up for themselves and for the people. They have the hands that carry the torch of hope, radiating beyond horizons. The motivated feet that go above and beyond just to find justice. The truthful heart, powered by their sincere passion and dedication, to serve willingly and to set people free.

Their battles are not similar to the ones people watch on screen. Their task to give people the truth and justice they're entitled to makes them risk their lives every day. Think about it, whenever there is a calamity, we see them in front of the cameras, reporting to their duty, destroyed infrastructures and fallen trees are seen behind them. Whenever there is an unfortunate event, we see them covered up with bulletproof vests, still gathering facts to create news to be broadcast. Whenever there is an election, no matter how many stares and dirty looks they receive, they'll still choose to inform people about the accurate results. Their battles don't consist of flaming swords and explosive powers, instead, they consist of bravery, intellect, and commitment.

It is very important for these heroes to find their weapons to combat one of their greatest opponents - fake news. Reliable and factual information is what sets the nation free from the chains of accusations. There have been times that due to lack of evidence, innocent people were put behind bars without getting to express their side of the story. Also, the people of the country, when their minds are not nurtured with the correct information, become prisoners of fake news. Therefore, it is a must for the heroes to act as soon as possible, in order to protect and guide the people, and so that the promising future that's ahead of us doesn't disappear into thin air.

These heroes are worthy of tribute and recognition, for no amount of money or gold is enough to commend their great service and resiliency. They are one of the proofs that kindness is present in any part of the world. They may not possess extraordinary abilities, but with their courageous mindset and their will to bring good change to our nation, they keep on fighting for the freedom of our country and its people. Truly, not all heroes wear capes.

A warrior, a protector, a conqueror, whatever you call it. The legacy they are making as the heroes of today's world is unmatched. They have the capabilities to move mountains and to make the world a better place. It is never too late to reawaken the spirits of countrymen to help fight against injustice. It is never too late to show our concern to our fellow. It is never too late for good change to happen.

Our writers. Our broadcasters. Our journalists. Our heroes.

Thank God for Teachers!

It was Master Oogway of the all-time fave "Kung Fu Panda" who struck my attention when he uttered, "Yesterday is history, tomorrow is a mystery, but today is a gift, that is why it is called the present." Indeed, we have one of the most precious gifts from above - yesterday, in the future, and at present. And they are called... teachers.

Teachers have an immeasurable amount of patience and love for learners. They make a lot of sacrifices for the sake of others. They dedicate their lives to making one a better person. They are the beacons of light who lead their learners towards the path of righteousness. They use their wings to carry people and put them to the pinnacle of success. Teachers nourish the minds of learners, and they leave an imprint that will never be erased in everyone's hearts.

I have always wanted to be a teacher. When I talk about this dream of mine, I would suddenly become a head-turner. People would then ask me the reason why I want to become a teacher. They get so curious to the point that they would even ask me if I had the patience or the capacity to handle the responsibilities of a teacher.

People thought I wanted to be a teacher just because I was born into a family of teachers. My parents are both passionate educators. As a kid, I was always astonished by the enormous amount of gifts they would receive on every occasion. And the little I wanted to be a teacher in order to experience such a thing. However, when innocence left my mind and I had already grown up, I realized that being a teacher didn't feel like sleeping in a bed of roses. As a daughter of teachers, I had witnessed their dedication to their chosen profession. I am a witness to the uncountable sacrifices they made. I could see my parents, staying up at night, finishing paperwork and preparing learning materials for their classes for the upcoming day. There were times when we weren't able to spend time together due to the call of service. Despite the adjustments and challenges my parents faced in their careers, they remained resilient, which made them remarkable teachers who are very much loved by their students. I am very proud to say that my parents are teachers. And yes, I want to follow in their footsteps.

As a student, I have also witnessed the greatness and unconditional love teachers offer to their students. They serve as students' second parents and look out for their students in a parently way. They take care of their students from the moment they come to the school to the time they leave. Rain or shine, regardless of the ups and downs, they conquered and delivered quality education to students. They were the ones who honed my skills and turned a stone like me into something close to a diamond. They stayed with me through thick and thin, helped me win the battles of my life, reminded me to keep my feet on the ground, and motivated me throughout my academic journey.

I owe everything to my teachers. Without them, I am a student whose quill does not bleed, a student whose dreams are colorless, and a person whose life doesn't have any inspiration. Teachers give their all in order to bring out the best in every student - they may sometimes have tiredness in their eyes and may think that they aren't contributing anything to the world at all, but little do they know, they are our inspirations and the people behind every goal and success. After all, they are our bravest warriors, our most determined workers, and the people who turn our dreams to reality.

As a way of giving back to them, I will and must give priority to my education. I will show my deepest and purest respect and gratitude to them. I commit every craft and achievement of mine to my teachers, and to pay tribute to them. When the time comes, I will also be the one to comfort, love, and inspire. When the time comes, I'll also be the one dressed in a uniform, talking in front of the class, and serve as an inspiration to the young minds. I will be a teacher. Not just because of the blood that flows through my veins, not just because of the gifts, not just for recognition. I will be a teacher, to be able to cultivate young minds and harness their skills to build a brighter future for the people and the generations to come.

To our dear teachers, we salute you and we are grateful for your commitment and efforts to your profession. The impact that you have on the youth is incomparable. May you never lose the will to continue serving the country and the learners. Now I understand why you are called the “Master of All Professions”, for behind every success, are unsung heroes. You may not always be recognized, but your essence remains real. Your legacy will always continue to live on, and will forever be treasured.

Thank God for teachers!

Chapter 6

Commitments *(Dreams and Responsibilities)*

TAPESTRY: Beauty in Diversity

On a usual busy morning, there was only heat and noise lurking around the four corners of our clothing shop. Yes, the art of sewing and creating traditional dresses runs in our family's blood. As the Gen-Z I am, who gets more restless when not occupied with something to work with, I decided to open one of my grandmother's *baul*. As I lay my eyes on the different objects inside it, I found treasures preserved by time. After looking through old sewing materials, I found a cloth - made up of threads from cotton balls, each thread contributing to form a design to make a cultural masterpiece. It was a product of Abel, the textile culture of Ilocandia.

Ilocandia is a melting pot of various cultures - from the highlanders to the lowlanders; to the different ethnic groups and indigenous people; to the multitude of flavors reflected in Ilocano cuisines; to the signature values such as austerity, courage, creativity, and the like; the God-given talents that dominate the international arena; and the deep sense of unity that dwells in every Ilocano's heart.

An Ilocano always says "YES" for good change.

An Ilocano **YEARN**S. Ilocandia is composed of different voices and aspirations that yearn for change. Ethnic groups like *Isnegs*, *Kalinga*, and *Igorots*, are living evidence of how innovative and knowledgeable Ilocanos are. They pour their hearts out in finding ways in order for them to thrive and survive. Even though they sometimes encounter obstacles, they still maintain a positive outlook towards life. **They hope. They work. They achieve**.

Furthermore, Ilocanos make foods as savory as every Ilocano's victory. Cuisines such as *pinakbet*, *sinanglao*, and *empanada,* showcase the variety of ingredients and spices Ilocanos use in order to produce great aroma and a tasty food served on top of the table, shared by the members of an Ilocano family. An Ilocano's time with family is something they wouldn't trade for anything. They always make sure that they don't leave their family hanging by a piece of a thread. **They make sacrifices. They dedicate their efforts. They find ways.**

An Ilocano **EARN**S. Ilocanos have soft hearts but firm desires. They don't only make you visit their place with a smile, but also amazes you with the desirable attributes they have. They are known for possessing austerity, courage, and creativity. They make use of their wits in order to get a better job and a better life. They value every penny and believe that money must be spent wisely. Ilocanos go above and beyond to achieve their needs, and save some for what they want. Even though they live a simple life, they extend their arms, ready to help those in need. **They prosper. They share. They uplift.**

An Ilocano **SUBMIT**S. Ilocanos are bestowed talents and strength in which they use to bring pride and glory to Ilocandia. From having Paulina Rangcapan, known as Nana Paul, who is the *damili* icon of San Nicolas; to Edgar Madamba, an international fashion designer, who crafted the *balimbing* cut silhouette of a Filipiniana; to Teofilo Yldefonso, who got the olympic arena to be shouting of joy; and to the Ilocano heroes who fought for the country's freedom - Gen. Artemio Ricarte, the Luna brothers, Gabriella Silang, and Josefa Llanes Escoda. These Ilocanos shed their blood and tears just to triumphantly bring change and laurels to the whole Ilocandia.

In fact, the common characteristic of Ilocanos, being God-fearing, became their common ground. All of their efforts and contributions to the Philippines of today, were dedications of them to the One True God. Ilocanos entrust everything, even their lives, to the Lord. For they have strong faith in Him, that will lead them to a better and brighter future. **They fight. They triumph. They pray.**

It is the resilience, bravery, and unconditional love for Ilocandia that makes an Ilocano a true one. Many threats may come their way, but never will they go in their shells and hide. Instead, they will fight the battle and be willing to sacrifice their lives to defend their dear Ilocandia. Being a fighter is hard, for you may be offered money or have a gun towards you. But with the Ilocano pride, no bullet can pass through and no amount of money will be able to bribe you.

A tapestry, filled with different hues and shapes, telling stories of culture and heritage throughout the years. A tapestry, in order to be magnificent, needs to be reflected with a variety of colors. A tapestry symbolizes Ilocandia. The secret in creating a stronger Ilocandia is not money or fame, but it lies in the unity of its people. It is given that Ilocanos may come from different roots, but we must not lose heart to nurture these once again, with the right water. Unison can be achieved when diversity is acknowledged and respected. If done correctly, we will come to learn that there is beauty in diversity.

As I finish reminiscing about the Ilocano culture while holding the cloth close to my chest, a thought comes to mind - this Inabel is never getting hidden again. It must be shown to the real world. Therefore, I will ask my mother to make a dress out of this Inabel cloth for me. My Ilocano heart will be very proud to wear it and showcase the beauty of Ilocano culture. I will be forever grateful to my ancestors for instilling the Ilocano blood in me. And I will do everything in my power, as a youth, to help weave the Ilocandia together, as one.

I am proud to be **unique**. I am proud to be **diverse**. YES, I am proud to be an **Ilocano**.

A Gentle Reminder: How to be a Good Athlete

Everyone who has interest in playing sports aspires to be a good athlete. They aspire to bear the torch that shines beyond horizons. They dream, they train, and they hope to succeed. But really, what does it take to be a good athlete?

Some say it depends on who's training you or what training did you undergo. Some say that it's a matter of luck. In order to give a conclusion to the aforementioned question, allow me to relate the growth of a student athlete to the process of pottery or Panagdamili. After all, we are San Nicoleños.

The first step would be preparing the materials needed and mixing the clay. When related to sports, it would mean to harness skills and show eagerness in flourishing athletic prowess. This is the time wherein student athletes come to discover their interests, and eventually want to compete for the school. They need to have courage and confidence to set their foot and take their first step on their athletic journey. Regardless of their fears and doubts, they bravely take on the challenge to proudly raise the banner of their schools high. They must prepare, trust, and allow themselves to grow.

Now that the clay is mixed, it must be molded. This is where the vital role that the coaches pay comes to the frame. In order to be a good athlete, open-mindedness must be possessed. Athletes must be ready and open to hear and abide by their coaches' suggestions and teachings in order for them to improve the way they play their games. Just like the potters, coaches are very hands-on, and will patiently mold them to turn out as fine and skilled athletes who are ready to dominate the sports arena.

Last but not the least, it is the firing process. It is when the athletes are entering the real game. The fire in the firing process makes the earthen pot resilient and harder to break. Athletes are just like the banga. The fire that symbolizes the obstacles and their experiences, builds their personalities and enhances their sportsmanship. WIn or lose, it is all a part of their growth. And when the time comes that they have reached the pinnacle of success, a good athlete will always remember to look back from where he came from, and to keep his feet on the ground.

The Triangular Meet 2023 had surely ignited the passion and love of athletes for sports. We hope that the experiences and lessons they have attained in this year's Triangular Meet will be used as their inspirations and will remain in their memory lane. We are sure that everyone did and gave their best.

San Nicolas student athletes, you all are winners. May you always be like the banga - resilient and able to withstand the flames of the challenges that you may encounter while venturing in your athletic journey. May you take the banga as your reminder to strive and be good and disciplined athletes. And we hope that with this year's Trangular Meet, you were able to realize the real essence of being an athlete. The real essence of being a San Nicoleño.

Ink of the Quill

A journalist is not only a writer, a cartoonist, or a broadcaster. In order for them to be role models and effectively make the truth prevail, there are essential Filipino values they need to project.

First is the value of humility. A journalist with a heart passionate about the truth has empathy for the people who deserve it. A journalist doesn't only serve himself and his agency, but rather, the whole country. Journalists, in order to serve their fellow Filipinos, must learn how to respect them, communicate with them, and be down to earth. No one can hold their fellows' hands if they are too high to reach. They should write every article with humility, broadcast every video with respect, and present their stands while prioritizing morals.

Next is the value of determination. Being a journalist is never an easy job. It comes with responsibilities, and these must be fulfilled with courage and sustained with commitment. A journalist doesn't give up just because of a minor inconvenience. He doesn't stop searching for the truth just because of a negative comment or a discouraging opinion. He doesn't stop informing the world with the latest updates just because of the powerful winds and heavy rains, the mighty shakes of earthquakes, and the explosive cannons during the war. A journalist, whose goals are aligned with his principles, can never be broken or taken down.

At last, it is the value of honesty. People are always given two choices in life – to do what’s good or to do what's bad. As journalists, their eyes are always set on the option in which the country will benefit from. Even with the endless threats, the big amounts of money, and the numerous offers of luxuries, journalists stand firm with integrity, not favoring one side over another. Journalists remain faithful and honest to their sworn oath and responsibility that is to provide responsive service, present unbiased news, and dedicate or sacrifice their lives for the sake of the country and its people.

A journalist is not only someone who appears right in front of the camera, whose names are written in the by-lines of news articles. They are our warriors who continue to battle against fake news, the bearers of truth, and the key-holders for us to unlock the threshold of success.

We salute you and your unwavering humility, determination, and honesty, Journalists!

ABOUT THE AUTHOR

Precious Kylee C. Bernardo is a young luminary born on March 13, 2009, into the nurturing embrace of two devoted educators, Mr. Rolly T. Bernardo and Mrs. Josie C. Bernardo. From the tender age of two, she embarked on her journey through nursery education, where the seeds of her love for writing were first sown, blossoming as she grasped the fundamentals of penmanship.

Throughout her formative years, Precious was enveloped in the guidance and inspiration of her educators, shaping her into an academic standout. Her innate talents caught the eye of her mentors, propelling her into the spotlight as she represented her school in a myriad of competitions. In 2018, as a third-grader, she made her debut in the Division Schools Press Conference, showcasing her prowess as a feature writer in Filipino Collaborative Writing and Desktop Publishing.

Undeterred by challenges, Precious continued to push the boundaries of her abilities, transitioning to compete individually in Feature Writing in English, ultimately advancing to the Regional Schools Press Conference—an achievement she repeated in subsequent years.

Venturing into high school at San Nicolas National High School, Precious seamlessly integrated into the Online Publishing English team, leaving an indelible mark as a news and feature writer. Their recent triumph, securing 2nd Place in the 2024 Regional Schools Press Conference, stands as a testament to her unwavering dedication and talent.

Beyond her accolades in campus journalism, Precious is a beacon of leadership, wielding her influence as an officer within her school's organizational framework. A voracious reader and aspiring author, she harbors a deep-seated passion for literature and storytelling, nurturing dreams of shaping young minds as a future educator.

Yet, amidst her individual achievements, Precious remains grounded in her roles as a loving daughter, a respectful student, and a compassionate friend. Her altruistic spirit shines through in her desire to uplift children and pave the way for their future—a testament to her boundless empathy and generosity of heart.

In every facet of her being, Precious embodies a mosaic of influences and legacies, a reflection of the diverse passions, learnings, and smiles that have shaped her journey. With her pen as her paintbrush, she continues to craft her masterpiece, driven by a singular goal: the pursuit of her own betterment and the empowerment of those around her.

Here is a list of her accomplishments as a student writer:

2nd Place
Feature Writing English
2018 District Schools Press Conference
San Nicolas, Ilocos Norte

2nd Place
Feature Writing English
2018 Division Schools Press Conference
Sarrat, Ilocos Norte

3rd Place
English Essay Writing - Elementary

UP Namnama Sirib ken Saririt 2019 Provincial Eliminations
City of Batac, Ilocos Norte

3rd Place
English Essay Writing - Elementary
UP Namnama Sirib ken Saririt 2019 Regional Finals
San Nicolas, Ilocos Norte

2nd Place
Feature Writing English
2019 District Schools Press Conference
San Nicolas, Ilocos Norte

2nd Place
Feature Writing English
2019 Division Schools Press Conference
Vintar, Ilocos Norte

2nd Place
English Essay Writing - Elementary
UP Namnama Sirib ken Saririt 2020 Provincial Eliminations
Vintar, Ilocos Norte

3rd Place
English Essay Writing - Elementary
UP Namnama Sirib ken Saririt 2020 Regional Finals
Baguio City

Participant
2021 Regional Schools Press Conference

Champion
Reading Challenge-JHS
School-Based Reading Month Celebration
San Nicolas National High School

1st Place
Online Publishing English
2023 Division Schools Press Conference
San Nicolas, Ilocos Norte

6.5th Place
Online Publishing English
2023 Regional Schools Press Conference
Alaminos City, Pangasinan

2nd Place
English Essay Writing - Junior High School
UP Namnama Sirib ken Saririt 2023 Provincial Eliminations

2nd Place
English Essay Writing - Junior High School
UP Namnama Sirib ken Saririt 2023 Regional Finals

Champion
Essay Writing Contest - Junior High School
School-Based Reading Month Celebration cum English Festival
San Nicolas National High School

1st Place
Essay Writing Contest
Feast Day of St. Nicholas de Tolentino Celebration
San Nicolas, Ilocos Norte

2nd Place
English Essay Writing - Junior High School
UP Namnama Sirib ken Saririt 2024 Provincial Eliminations

2nd Place
English Essay Writing - Junior High School
UP Namnama Sirib ken Saririt 2024 Regional Finals

1st Place
Online Publishing English
2024 Division Schools Press Conference
San Nicolas, Ilocos Norte

2nd Place
Online Publishing English
2024 Regional Schools Press Conference
Vigan City, Ilocos Sur

1st Place
Essay Writing Contest
2024 School-Based International Day of Mathematics Celebration
San Nicolas National High School

1st Place
One-Act Play Writing (SULATANGHAL)
2024 Division Festival of Talents
Solsona, Ilocos Norte

www.ingramcontent.com/pod-product-compliance
Lightning Source LLC
LaVergne TN
LVHW020036170826
845678LV00001B/280

* 9 7 8 6 2 1 4 9 5 0 9 8 0 *